Trumpe

Written by Meredith Costain
Illustrated by Sue O'Loughlin

sundance

a black dog book

Published by
Sundance Publishing
P.O. Box 1326
234 Taylor Street
Littleton, MA 01460

First published 2001 by
Pearson Education Australia Pty. Limited
95 Coventry Street
South Melbourne 3205 Australia
Exclusive United States Distribution: Sundance Publishing

ISBN 0-7608-4978-1

Printed in China

Contents

Characters

Dex loves music.
He likes to hum
his favorite songs
whenever he can.

Alex loves music, too.
He likes to play
loud instruments.

Chapter One

Music Class

Dex hummed as he raced along the hall. He waved to Mr. Mead, the school custodian. Mr. Mead waved back.

It was Tuesday. Every Tuesday, Dex's class had music with Mr. Franklin.

Dex liked all kinds of music. He liked pop songs and rock songs and rap songs. But most of all, he liked playing the trumpet in music class.

Mr. Franklin came into the room, carrying a huge box. Dex knew exactly what was in that box—musical instruments. Shakers that rattled. Cymbals that clanged. Recorders that tooted. And an old, silver trumpet, full of dents.

“Good morning, class,” Mr. Franklin said. “I’ve got some news. We’re putting on a school concert.”

Dex’s eyes flew open. Fantastic! Now he’d get a chance to play the trumpet for lots of people.

Mr. Franklin passed around the instruments. Everyone chose one. Dex's friend, Jamie, chose bongo drums. Whitney chose cymbals. Amy chose a recorder.

"I want the trumpet," said Alex Winter.

Dex's heart skipped a beat. When Alex played the trumpet, it made a noise like a sick cow. Mr. Franklin couldn't give the trumpet to Alex, could he? But he did.

Finally it was Dex's turn to choose. He looked down at the leftover instruments—three triangles and a wooden shaker.

"What would you like to play, Dex?" asked Mr. Franklin.

Dex looked at Alex Winter. Alex was laughing and waving the trumpet. Dex looked back at Mr. Franklin. "Doesn't matter," Dex sighed. "I don't care."

Mr. Franklin handed Dex a triangle. Then he winked. "Come to my office after class, Dex," he said. "I may have something you'll like."

Chapter Two

The Special Trumpet

After class, Dex went to Mr. Franklin's office. Mr. Franklin was waiting for him. He held a gleaming trumpet in his hand.

“You really wanted that trumpet today, didn’t you, Dex,” said Mr. Franklin.

“Yes,” whispered Dex. He was trying not to think about Alex Winter and his sick-cow noises.

Mr. Franklin handed the trumpet to Dex. “Well, now you’ve got one, too. This is my own trumpet. It’s very special to me. I’m lending it to you so you can practice. You can bring it to class next Tuesday. Take good care of it.”

Dex looked at the trumpet. It was beautiful. The metal was smooth and shiny. It looked like real gold. Dex was so excited that it took him a moment to speak. "Thank you, Mr. Franklin. I will take care of it. You can count on me."

"Good," said Mr. Franklin. "And make sure you practice like mad."

Dex turned the gleaming trumpet over and over in his hands. This trumpet was much better than the old school trumpet. He blew into the mouthpiece. The trumpet sounded bright and colorful, like a circus. He blew another note. This time the trumpet sounded sad, like a rainy day.

Chapter Three
Practicing Like Mad

Dex put the trumpet carefully in his bag. This was the most awesome thing that had ever happened to him.

Dex was going to practice like mad. He would be the best trumpet player ever. His class would put on the greatest concert. He would make a CD and give a copy to everyone in his family.

At the end of morning recess, Dex couldn't resist. He opened his bag, just to make sure the trumpet was real.

“Wow!” said Jamie, peeking into the bag. “Can I play it?”

“Just for a minute,” said Dex. Mr. Franklin hadn’t said Dex could lend the special trumpet to anyone. But he hadn’t said that Dex couldn’t, either.

Jamie blew hard into the mouthpiece. "Brrummmphh!" went the trumpet.

"Not so loud!" whispered Dex. "Everyone will want to play it."

But it was too late.

"Hey!" said Alex Winter. "Let me play that trumpet!"

"No," said Dex, trying to grab the trumpet. But Alex had already snatched it.

Just then, Mrs. Liston stormed into the room. “What’s all of this noise?” she asked.

Everyone stopped talking. Dex tried to sneak the trumpet back into his bag.

“Dexter Harris,” said Mrs. Liston. “Bring that to me.”

Dex handed the trumpet to Mrs. Liston. She placed it on her desk. "This noisy thing can stay here," she said.

The day seemed to drag on forever. Dex couldn't think about schoolwork. He couldn't think about anything at all, except the trumpet.

Finally the bell rang. Mrs. Liston checked her watch. "Time to go home," she announced.

"Excuse me, Mrs. Liston," said Dex. "What about my trumpet?"

"The trumpet stays here," said Mrs. Liston. "You can have it in the morning."

"But—" said Dex.

"It doesn't have legs, does it?" said Mrs. Liston. "It can't go anywhere."

Dex grabbed his bag from its hook and sadly began the walk home. Mr. Franklin wanted him to practice like mad. The last thing he ever wanted to do was let Mr. Franklin down.

Chapter Four
First in Line

The next morning, Dex was first in line to enter the classroom. As soon as Mrs. Liston arrived, he rushed inside and went straight to her desk.

The trumpet was gone! Dex's heart was beating very fast. He peeked under Mrs. Liston's desk. He looked behind the bookshelves. He peered inside the wastebasket and under the projects on the science table.

No trumpet. But he tried not to panic.

“Has anyone seen my trumpet?” Dex asked.

But nobody knew where it was—not even Alex Winter.

Chapter Five

The Missing Trumpet

Dex tried really hard to find the trumpet. He looked everywhere.

He checked the Lost and Found box in the office.

He even used a metal detector.

Every day, Dex and Jamie searched the school. They searched from top to bottom. They found lots of stuff, but they didn't find the trumpet.

"What are you going to tell Mr. Franklin?" Jamie asked Dex.

Dex hung his head. Mr. Franklin had trusted him. And now the special trumpet was gone.

The most awesome thing that had ever happened had turned out to be the most awful thing. Dex never wanted to see a trumpet again.

Chapter Six
Found at Last

On Tuesday, Dex tiptoed into music class. He sat at the back of the room and hoped Mr. Franklin wouldn't notice him.

Mr. Franklin put the instrument box on his desk. “Okay, everyone, let’s get started,” he said.

One by one, the kids found their instruments. Dex saw Alex Winter reach into the box and pull out the old school trumpet. Then Jamie looked into the box.

“Hey, Dex!” shouted Jamie. “Look what’s in here!”

“The trumpet!” shouted Dex.

“My trumpet!” shouted Mr. Franklin. “How did it get in there?”

“Yes, how?” whispered Dex. A noise outside made him look out the window. Mr. Mead was sweeping leaves.

“Excuse me, Mr. Franklin,” Dex asked politely. “Can I go outside to talk to Mr. Mead for a minute?”

Mr. Franklin looked puzzled. “Sure, Dex,” he said. “But come straight back.”

Moments later, Dex returned to class with Mr. Mead.

"I was playing the trumpet in Mrs. Liston's class. So Mrs. Liston took it," Dex told Mr. Franklin. "Mr. Mead found it on Mrs. Liston's desk."

"I thought the trumpet had been left out by mistake," explained Mr. Mead. "So I put it in the instrument box."

Mr. Franklin smiled. Then he handed the trumpet to Dex. "You'd better start practicing like mad, Dex," he said. "Only two weeks until the concert. But try not to play it in Mrs. Liston's class."

Dex played a note. "Brrummmphh!" The trumpet sounded like a carnival. Dex couldn't wait to play it on stage.

"Don't worry, Mr. Franklin," he said. "You can count on me!"